C

APPROVED RITES FOR USE IN
THE UNITED STATES OF AMERICA
EXCERPTED FROM
PASTORAL CARE OF THE SICK
AND DYING
IN ENGLISH AND SPANISH

INCLUDING AN APPENDIX WITH
HISTORY AND COMMENTARY
BY REVEREND JOSEPH M. CHAMPLIN

C. B.   P. C.

CATHOLIC BOOK PUBLISHING CORP.
NEW JERSEY

Published with the approval of the
Committee on Divine Worship,
United States Conference of Catholic Bishops

(T-82)

ISBN 978-0-89942-082-0

CONTENTS

Prayer for Extraordinary Ministers of Holy Communion

LORD Jesus Christ,
You are the Word of God and Bread of Life.

Help me to bring your gospel message
and Eucharistic Presence to others.

Help me to do so with faith and reverence,
with love and concern.

May I carry out this sacred ministry
comfortably, but not casually,
relaxed, yet with awesome respect.

All praise to you,
the God who is, who was, and
who is to come
at the end of the ages.

COMMUNION IN ORDINARY CIRCUMSTANCES

INTRODUCTION

Whoever eats this bread will live for ever.

71   This booklet contains two rites: one for use when Communion can be celebrated in the context of a Liturgy of the Word; the other, a brief Communion rite for use in more restrictive circumstances, such as in hospitals.

72   Priests with pastoral responsibilities should see to it that the sick or aged, even though not seriously ill or in danger of death, are given every opportunity to receive the Eucharist frequently, even daily, especially during Easter Time. They may receive Communion at any hour. Those who care for the sick may receive Communion with them, in accord with the usual norms. To provide frequent Communion for the sick, it may be necessary to ensure that the community has a sufficient number of extraordinary ministers of Holy Communion. The minister should wear attire appropriate to this ministry.

    The sick person and others may help to plan the celebration, for example, by choosing the prayers and readings. Those making these choices should keep in mind the condition of the sick person. The readings and the homily should help those present to reach a deeper understanding of the mystery of human suffering in relation to the Paschal Mystery of Christ.

73   The faithful who are ill are deprived of their rightful and accustomed place in the Eucharistic community.

In bringing Communion to them the extraordinary minister of Holy Communion represents Christ and manifests faith and charity on behalf of the whole community toward those who cannot be present at the Eucharist. For the sick the reception of Communion is not only a privilege but also a sign of support and concern shown by the Christian community for its members who are ill.

The links between the community's Eucharistic celebration, especially on the Lord's Day, and the Communion of the sick are intimate and manifold. Besides remembering the sick in the Universal Prayer at Mass, those present should be reminded occasionally of the significance of Communion in the lives of those who are ill: union with Christ in his struggle with evil, his prayer for the world, and his love for the Father, and union with the community from which they are separated.

The obligation to visit and comfort those who cannot take part in the Eucharistic assembly may be clearly demonstrated by taking Communion to them from the community's Eucharistic celebration. This symbol of unity between the community and its sick members has the deepest significance on the Lord's Day, the special day of the Eucharistic assembly.

74   When the Eucharist is brought to the sick, it should be carried in a pyx or small closed container. Those who are with the sick should be asked to prepare a table covered with a linen cloth upon which the Blessed Sacrament will be placed. Lighted candles are prepared and, where it is customary, a vessel of holy water. Care should be taken to make the occasion special and joyful.

Sick people who are unable to receive Communion under the form of bread may receive it under the form of wine alone. If the wine is consecrated at a Mass not celebrated in the presence of the sick person, the Blood of the Lord is kept in a properly covered vessel and is placed in the tabernacle after Communion. The Precious Blood should be carried to the sick in a vessel which is closed in such a way as to eliminate all danger of spilling. If some of the Precious Blood remains, it should be consumed by the minister, who should also see to it that the vessel is properly purified afterward by a Priest or Deacon.

75   If the sick wish to celebrate the Sacrament of Penance, it is preferable that the Priest make himself available for this during a previous visit.

76   If it is necessary to celebrate the Sacrament of Penance during the rite of Communion, it takes the place of the Penitential Act.

OUTLINE OF THE RITE

INTRODUCTORY RITES

Greeting
Sprinkling with Holy Water
Penitential Act

LITURGY OF THE WORD

Reading
Response
Universal Prayer

LITURGY OF HOLY COMMUNION

The Lord's Prayer
Communion
Silent Prayer
Prayer after Communion

CONCLUDING RITE

Blessing

INTRODUCTORY RITES

GREETING

81   The minister greets the sick person and the others present. One of the following may be used:

A

Minister: **Peace be with this house and with all who live here.**

B

Minister: **The peace of the Lord be with you.**

C

Minister: **The grace of our Lord Jesus Christ,
and the love of God,
and the communion of the Holy Spirit
be with you all.**

D

Minister: **Grace to you and peace from God our Father
and the Lord Jesus Christ.**

If the minister is a Priest or Deacon, all respond: **And with your spirit**.

If the minister is not a Priest or Deacon, he or she adds to the greeting: **Blessed be God for ever**, to which all respond: **Blessed be God for ever**.

The minister then places the Blessed Sacrament on the table, and all join in adoration.

Sprinkling with Holy Water

82   If it seems desirable, the Priest or Deacon may sprinkle the sick person and those present with holy water. One of the following may be used:

A

Let this water call to mind our Baptism into Christ, who by his Death and Resurrection has redeemed us.

B

Like a stream in parched land,
may the grace of the Lord
refresh our lives.

If the Sacrament of Penance is now celebrated, the Penitential Act is omitted.

Penitential Act

83   The minister invites the sick person and all present to join in the Penitential Act, using these or similar words:

A

My brothers and sisters, to prepare ourselves for this celebration, let us call to mind our sins.

B

My brothers and sisters, let us turn with confidence to the Lord and ask his forgiveness for all our sins.

After a brief period of silence, the Penitential Act continues, using one of the following:

A

All say:

I confess to almighty God
and to you, my brothers and sisters,
that I have greatly sinned,
in my thoughts and in my words,
in what I have done and in what I have failed
 to do,

And, striking their breast, they say:

through my fault, through my fault,
through my most grievous fault;

Then they continue:

therefore I ask blessed Mary ever-Virgin,
all the Angels and Saints,
and you, my brothers and sisters,
to pray for me to the Lord our God.

B

Minister: **Have mercy on us, O Lord.**

All: For we have sinned against you.

Minister: **Show us, O Lord, your mercy.**

All: And grant us your salvation.

C

Minister: **Lord Jesus, you healed the sick:**
Lord, have mercy.

All: Lord, have mercy.

Minister: **Lord, Jesus, you forgave sinners:**
Christ, have mercy.

All: Christ, have mercy.

Minister: **Lord Jesus, you give us yourself to heal**
us and bring us strength:
Lord, have mercy.

All: Lord, have mercy.

The minister concludes the Penitential Act with the following:

May almighty God have mercy on us,
forgive us our sins,
and bring us to everlasting life.

All: Amen.

LITURGY OF THE WORD

READING

84   The word of God is proclaimed by one of those present or by the minister. One of the following readings or another biblical passage may be used:

                                          John 6:51

✠ **A reading from the holy Gospel**
according to John

Jesus says:
  "I am the living bread that came down from
    heaven;
  whoever eats this bread will live forever;

and the bread that I will give
is my Flesh for the life of the world."

The Gospel of the Lord.

B   John 6:54-58

✠ A reading from the holy Gospel
according to John

Jesus says:
"Whoever eats my Flesh and drinks my Blood
has eternal life,
and I will raise him on the last day.
For my Flesh is true food,
and my Blood is true drink.
Whoever eats my Flesh and drinks my Blood
remains in me and I in him.
Just as the living Father sent me
and I have life because of the Father,
so also the one who feeds on me
will have life because of me.
This is the bread that came down from heaven.
Unlike your ancestors who ate and still died,
whoever eats this bread will live forever."

The Gospel of the Lord.

C   John 14:6

✠ A reading from the holy Gospel
according to John

Jesus says:
"I am the way and the truth and the life.
No one comes to the Father except through me."

The Gospel of the Lord.

D   John 15:5

✠ A reading from the holy Gospel
according to John

Jesus says:
"I am the vine, you are the branches.
Whoever remains in me and I in him will bear
much fruit,
because without me you can do nothing."

The Gospel of the Lord.

E   1 John 4:16

A reading from the first Letter of Saint John

We have come to know and to believe in the
love God has for us.

God is love, and whoever remains in love
remains in God and God in him.

The word of the Lord.

RESPONSE

85   A brief period of silence may be observed after the
reading of the word of God.

The minister may then give a brief explanation of the
reading, applying it to the needs of the sick person and
those who are looking after him or her.

Uɴɪᴠᴇʀsᴀʟ Pʀᴀʏᴇʀ

86   The Universal Prayer (Prayer of the Faithful) may
be said. With a brief introduction the minister invites all
those present to pray. After the intentions the minister
says the concluding prayer. It is desirable that the intentions be announced by someone other than the minister.
[See guidelines and suggestions on pp. 52-53.]

LITURGY OF HOLY COMMUNION

Tʜᴇ Lᴏʀᴅ's Pʀᴀʏᴇʀ

87   The minister introduces the Lord's Prayer in these
or similar words:

A

**Now let us pray as Christ the Lord has taught
us:**

B

**And now let us pray with confidence as Christ
our Lord commanded:**

All say:

  Our Father . . .

COMMUNION

88   The minister shows the Eucharistic Bread to those present, saying:

**Behold the Lamb of God,
behold him who takes away the sins of the world.
Blessed are those called to the supper of the Lamb.**

The sick person and all who are to receive Communion say:

> Lord, I am not worthy
> that you should enter under my roof,
> but only say the word
> and my soul shall be healed.

The minister goes to the sick person and, showing the Blessed Sacrament, says:

The Body of Christ.

(and/or **The Blood of Christ.**)

The sick person answers: **Amen**, and receives Communion.

Others present who wish to receive Communion then do so in the usual way.

After the conclusion of the rite, the minister cleanses the vessel as usual.

Silent Prayer

89 Then a period of silence may be observed.

Prayer after Communion

90 The minister says a concluding prayer. One of the following may be used:

Let us pray.

Pause for silent prayer, if this has not preceded.

All-powerful and ever-living God,
may the Body and Blood of Christ your Son
be for our brother/sister N.
a lasting remedy for body and soul.
Through Christ our Lord.

All: Amen.

B

O God, who have willed that we be partakers
in the one Bread and the one Chalice,
grant us, we pray, so to live
that, made one in Christ,
we may joyfully bear fruit
for the salvation of the world.
Through Christ our Lord.

All: Amen.

C

Nourished by this sacred gift, O Lord,
we give you thanks and beseech your mercy,
that, by the pouring forth of your Spirit,
the grace of integrity may endure
in those your heavenly power has entered.
Through Christ our Lord.

All: Amen.

CONCLUDING RITE

BLESSING

91   The Priest or Deacon blesses the sick person and
the others present, using one of the following blessings.
If, however, any of the Blessed Sacrament remains, he
may bless the sick person by making a Sign of the Cross
with the Blessed Sacrament, in silence.

A

Priest: **May God the Father bless you.**
All: Amen.

Priest: **May the Son of God heal you.**
All: Amen.

Priest: **May the Holy Spirit shed light upon you.**
All: Amen.

Priest: **May God guard your body and save your
         soul.**
All: Amen.

Priest: **May he enlighten your heart and lead you to life on high.**

All: Amen.

Priest: **And may almighty God bless all of you, who are gathered here,**
       the Father, and the Son, ✠ and the Holy Spirit.

All: Amen.

B

Priest: **May the Lord Jesus Christ be with you to defend you.**

All: Amen.

Priest: **May he go before you to lead you and behind you to guard you.**

All: Amen.

Priest: **May he look upon you, keep you safe and bless you.**

All: Amen.

Priest: **And may almighty God bless all of you, who are gathered here,**
       the Father, and the Son, ✠ and the Holy Spirit.

All: Amen.

C

Priest: **May the blessing of almighty God,**
       the Father, and the Son, ✠ and the Holy Spirit,
       come down on you and remain with you for ever.

All: Amen.

A minister who is not a Priest or Deacon invokes God's blessing and makes the Sign of the Cross on himself or herself, while saying:

A

Minister: **May the Lord bless us,**
protect us from all evil,
and bring us to everlasting life.

All: Amen.

B

Minister: **May the almighty and merciful God**
bless and protect us,
the Father, and the Son, and the Holy
Spirit.

All: Amen.

COMMUNION IN A HOSPITAL OR INSTITUTION

INTRODUCTION

78   There will be situations, particularly in large institutions with many communicants, when the minister should consider alternative means so that the rite of Communion of the sick is not diminished to the absolute minimum. In such cases the following alternatives should be considered: (a) where possible, the residents or patients may be gathered in groups in one or more areas; (b) additional ministers of Communion may assist.

When it is not possible to celebrate the full rite, the rite for Communion in a hospital or institution may be used. If it is convenient, however, the minister may add elements from the rite for ordinary circumstances, for example, a Scripture reading.

79   The rite begins with the recitation of the Eucharistic antiphon in the church, the hospital chapel, or the first room visited. Then the minister gives Communion to the sick in their individual rooms.

80   The concluding prayer may be said in the church, the hospital chapel, or the last room visited. No blessing is given.

OUTLINE OF THE RITE

INTRODUCTORY RITE
Antiphon

LITURGY OF HOLY COMMUNION
Greeting
The Lord's Prayer
Communion

CONCLUDING RITE
Concluding Prayer

INTRODUCTORY RITE

92   The rite may begin in the church, the hospital chapel, or the first room, where the minister says one of the following antiphons:

A

How holy this feast
in which Christ is our food:
his passion is recalled;
grace fills our hearts;
and we receive a pledge of the glory to come.

B

How gracious you are, Lord:
your gift of bread from heaven
reveals a Father's love and brings us perfect
  joy.
You fill the hungry with good things
and send the rich away empty.

C

I am the living bread
come down from heaven.
If you eat this bread
you will live for ever.
The bread I will give is my flesh
for the life of the world.

If it is customary, the minister may be accompanied by a person carrying a candle.

LITURGY OF HOLY COMMUNION

GREETING

93   On entering each room, the minister may use one of the following greetings:

Minister: **The peace of the Lord be with you.**

Minister: **The grace of our Lord Jesus Christ,
and the love of God,
and the communion of the Holy Spirit
be with you all.**

If the minister is a Priest or Deacon, all respond: **And with your spirit**.

If the minister is not a Priest or Deacon, he or she adds to the greeting: **Blessed be God for ever**, to which all respond: **Blessed be God for ever**.

The minister then places the Blessed Sacrament on the table, and all join in adoration.

If there is time and it seems desirable, the minister may proclaim a Scripture reading from those found on pages 12-14.

THE LORD'S PRAYER

94   When circumstances permit (for example, when there are not many rooms to visit), the minister is encouraged to lead the sick in the Lord's Prayer. The minister introduces the Lord's Prayer in these or similar words:

Jesus taught us to call God our Father, and so we have the courage to say:

Now let us pray as Christ the Lord has taught us:

All say:

> **Our Father . . .**

COMMUNION

95   The minister shows the Eucharistic Bread to those present, saying:

**Behold the Lamb of God,
behold him who takes away the sins of the world.
Blessed are those called to the supper of the Lamb.**

The sick person and all who are to receive Communion say:

> Lord, I am not worthy
> that you should enter under my roof,
> but only say the word
> and my soul shall be healed.

The minister goes to the sick person and, showing the Blessed Sacrament, says:

The Body of Christ.

(and/or **The Blood of Christ.**)

The sick person answers: **Amen**, and receives Communion.

Others present who wish to receive Communion then do so in the usual way.

CONCLUDING RITE

CONCLUDING PRAYER

96   The concluding prayer may be said either in the last room visited, in the church, or chapel. One of the following may be used.

Let us pray.

Pause for silent prayer.

All-powerful and ever-living God,
may the Body and Blood of Christ your Son
be for our brother/sister N.
a lasting remedy for body and soul.
Through Christ our Lord.

All: Amen.

B

O God, who have willed that we be partakers
in the one Bread and the one Chalice,
grant us, we pray, so to live
that, made one in Christ,
we may joyfully bear fruit
for the salvation of the world.
Through Christ our Lord.

All: Amen.

C

Nourished by this sacred gift, O Lord,
we give you thanks and beseech your mercy,
that, by the pouring forth of your Spirit,
the grace of integrity may endure
in those your heavenly power has entered.
Through Christ our Lord.

All: Amen.

The blessing is omitted and the minister cleanses the
vessel as usual.

COMUNIÓN EN CIRCUNSTANCIAS ORDINARIAS

●

COMUNIÓN EN UN HOSPITAL U OTRA INSTITUCIÓN

COMUNIÓN EN
CIRCUNSTANCIAS ORDINARIAS

ESQUEMA DEL RITO

RITOS INTRODUCTORIOS

Saludo
Aspersión con agua bendita
Rito penitencial

LITURGIA DE LA PALABRA

Lectura
Respuesta a la Palabra
Preces

LITURGIA DE LA COMUNIÓN

Oración dominical
Comunión
Oración en silencio
Oración después de la comunión

RITO CONCLUSIVO

Bendición

RITOS INTRODUCTORIOS

81 El ministro saluda a la persona enferma y a los presentes.

La paz del Señor esté siempre con ustedes.

℟. Y con tu espíritu.

Entonces el ministro coloca el Santísimo Sacramento en la mesa y todos juntos lo adoran.

ASPERSIÓN CON AGUA BENDITA

82 Si parece conveniente, el sacerdote o el diácono rocía con agua bendita a la persona enferma y a todos los presentes.

**Que esta agua bendita nos recuerde
el bautismo que recibimos
y renueve nuestra fe en Cristo,
que con su muerte y resurrección nos redimió.**

Si tiene lugar aquí el sacramento de la penitencia, se omite el rito penitencial.

RITO PENITENCIAL

83 El ministro invita a la persona enferma y a todos los presentes a participar en el rito penitencial, con estas u otras palabras parecidas:

**Hermanos y hermanas,
para prepararnos a esta celebración,
reconozcamos nuestros pecados.**

Después de un breve momento de silencio, prosigue el rito penitencial.

**Señor Jesús, que curaste a los enfermos:
Señor, ten piedad de nosotros.**

℟. Señor, ten piedad de nosotros.

**Señor Jesús, que perdonaste a los pecadores:
Cristo, ten piedad de nosotros.**

℟. Cristo, ten piedad de nosotros.

**Señor Jesús, que te entregaste a la muerte
para sanarnos y darnos fortaleza:
Señor, ten piedad de nosotros.**

℟. Señor, ten piedad de nosotros.

El ministro concluye el rito penitencial, diciendo:

**Dios todopoderoso tenga misericordia de nosotros,
perdone nuestros pecados
y nos lleve a la vida eterna.**

℟. Amén.

LITURGIA DE LA PALABRA

LECTURA

84   Uno de los presentes o el ministro proclama la palabra de Dios.

✠ **Lectura del santo Evangelio
según San Juan**   6.51

**Jesús dice:
"Yo soy el pan vivo que ha bajado del cielo:
el que coma de este pan vivirá para siempre.**

Y el pan que yo les voy a dar es mi carne
para que el mundo tenga vida".

Palabra del Señor.

✠ **Lectura del santo Evangelio
según San Juan**   14.6

Jesús dice:
"Yo soy el camino, la verdad y la vida.
Nadie va al Padre si no es por mí".

Palabra del Señor.

Respuesta a la Palabra

85   Se puede guardar un breve espacio de silencio,
después de la lectura de la palabra de Dios.

El ministro podrá explicar brevemente la lectura y
aplicarla a las necesidades de la persona enferma y de
los que cuidan de ella.

Preces

86   Se pueden enunciar las peticiones generales.
Mediante una breve introducción, el ministro invita a
todos a orar. Después de las intenciones, el ministro
recita la oración conclusiva. Es recomendable que una
persona distinta del ministro pronuncie las intenciones.

LITURGIA DE LA COMUNIÓN

Oración dominical

87   El ministro introduce la oración dominical con
estas o semejantes palabras:

Oremos confiadamente al Padre con las palabras que nos enseñó nuestro Salvador:

Todos dicen:

Padre nuestro . . .

COMUNIÓN

88 El ministro presenta el pan eucarístico a los presentes, con estas palabras:

Éste es el pan de la vida.
Prueben y vean qué bueno es el Señor.

La persona enferma y todos los que vayan a comulgar dicen:

Señor, no soy digno de que entres en mi casa, pero una palabra tuya bastará para sanarme.

El ministro se acerca a la persona enferma y presentándole el Santísimo Sacramento, dice:

El Cuerpo de Cristo.

La persona enferma responde: **Amén**, y recibe la comunión.

Si se da la comunión bajo la especie de vino, el ministro dice:

La Sangre de Cristo.

La persona enferma responde: **Amén**, y recibe la comunión.

Si otras personas quieren comulgar, pueden hacerlo en la forma acostumbrada.

Terminado el rito, el ministro purifica los vasos sagrados, como de costumbre.

Oración en Silencio

89   A continuación se puede guardar un momento de silencio.

Oración después de la Comunión

90   El ministro reza la oración conclusiva.

Oremos.

Pausa para orar en silencio, si no se ha hecho anteriormente.

Señor y Padre nuestro,
que nos has llamado a participar
del mismo pan y del mismo vino,
para vivir así unidos a Cristo,
ayúdanos a vivir unidos a él,
para que produzcamos fruto,
experimentando el gozo de su redención.
Por Jesucristo, nuestro Señor.

℟.   Amén.

RITO CONCLUSIVO

Bendición

91   El sacerdote o el diácono bendice a la persona enferma y a los presentes. Pero, si han quedado algunas formas consagradas, puede bendecir al enfermo, haciendo, en silencio, la señal de la cruz con el Santísimo Sacramento.

Que Dios Padre te bendiga.

℟. Amén.

Que Dios Hijo te cure.

℟. Amén.

Que Dios Espíritu Santo te ilumine.

℟. Amén.

**Que te bendiga Dios todopoderoso,
Padre, Hijo ✠ y Espíritu Santo.**

℟. Amén.

Si el ministro no es sacerdote ni diácono, invoca la bendición de Dios y hace sobre sí mismo(a) la señal de la cruz, diciendo:

**Que el Señor nos bendiga,
nos libre de todo mal
y nos lleve a la vida eterna.**

℟. Amén.

COMUNIÓN EN UN HOSPITAL U OTRA INSTITUCIÓN

ESQUEMA DEL RITO

RITO INTRODUCTORIO
Antífona

LITURGIA DE LA COMUNIÓN
Saludo
Oración dominical
Comunión

RITO CONCLUSIVO
Oración conclusiva

RITO INTRODUCTORIO

ANTÍFONA

92   El rito puede iniciarse en el templo, en la capilla del hospital o en el primer cuarto, en donde el sacerdote recita la siguiente antífona:

> **¡Oh sagrado banquete**
> **donde Cristo es alimento!**
> **Se recuerda su pasión,**
> **el alma se llena de gracia,**
> **y se nos da en prenda**
> **la gloria futura.**

Si se acostumbra, el ministro puede ir acompañado por una persona que lleve una vela.

LITURGIA DE LA COMUNIÓN

SALUDO

93   Al entrar en cada habitación, el ministro puede recitar el siguiente saludo:

> **Que la paz del Señor esté siempre con ustedes.**

℟. Y con tu espíritu.

El ministro coloca el Santísimo Sacramento en la mesa y todos juntos lo adoran.

Si hay tiempo y parece conveniente, el ministro puede proclamar la palabra.

ORACIÓN DOMINICAL

94   Si las circunstancias lo permiten (por ejemplo, si no son muchas las salas que hay que visitar), es muy conveniente que el ministro guíe a los enfermos en la recitación de la oración dominical. Puede hacerlo con estas o semejantes palabras:

> **Jesús nos enseñó a llamar Padre a Dios;**
> **por eso nos atrevemos a decir:**

Todos dicen:

> Padre nuestro . . .

COMUNIÓN

95   El ministro muestra el pan eucarístico a los presentes, diciendo:

> **Éste es el Cordero de Dios**
> **que quita el pecado del mundo.**
> **¡Dichosos los que tienen hambre y sed,**
> **porque ellos serán saciados!**

La persona enferma y todos aquellos que vayan a comulgar dicen:

Señor, no soy digno de que entres en mi casa, pero una palabra tuya bastará para sanarme.

El ministro se acerca a la persona enferma, le muestra el Santísimo Sacramento, diciéndole:

El Cuerpo de Cristo.

La persona enferma responde: **Amén**, y recibe la comunión.

Si se da la comunión bajo la especie de vino, el ministro dice:

La Sangre de Cristo.

La persona enferma responde: **Amén**, y recibe la comunión.

Si otras personas quieren comulgar, pueden hacerlo en la forma acostumbrada.

RITO CONCLUSIVO

ORACIÓN CONCLUSIVA

96   La oración conclusiva puede recitarse en el último salón o habitación o en la iglesia o en la capilla.

Oremos.

Pausa para orar en silencio.

> **Señor y Padre nuestro,**
> **que nos has llamado a participar**
> **del mismo pan y del mismo vino,**
> **para vivir así unidos a Cristo,**
> **ayúdanos a vivir unidos a él,**
> **para que produzcamos fruto,**
> **experimentando el gozo de su redención.**
> **Por Jesucristo, nuestro Señor.**
>
> ℟. Amén.

Se omite la bendición y el ministro purifica los vasos sagrados como de costumbre.

APPENDIX I

Beginning This Ministry

History

A HALF century ago, parish Priests expended a major portion of their time and energy bringing Holy Communion to the sick or homebound. Each Priest would have a list of a few or perhaps several dozen persons unable to participate in Mass at church. Usually once a month, often trying to make that visit on a First Friday, the clergy would call upon those ill or confined, carefully carrying the Blessed Sacrament to them.

This pattern changed radically and rapidly after January 29, 1973. At that time Pope Paul VI issued an instruction on "Facilitating Sacramental Communion in Particular Circumstances." This document and a subsequent section published for inclusion in the Roman Ritual, "Holy Communion and Worship of the Eucharist Outside Mass," approved extraordinary ministers of Holy Communion.

Where insufficient numbers of ordinary ministers (Priests or Deacons) existed, trained and commissioned laypersons were now allowed to assist at Mass with the distribution of Holy Communion and to bring the Eucharistic Lord to those confined at home because of illness or other factors.

There was an immediate and swift implementation of those decrees in the United States. Within a mere decade extraordinary ministers of Holy Communion numbered in the hundreds of thousands. It would, to illustrate, not be uncommon today for a large parish to list 150 people in this category. Moreover, the development of a ministry for laypersons bringing Communion to the sick took on a remarkable, inspiring and positive life of its own.

Laypersons began to carry the Eucharistic Lord to those confined at home on a more frequent basis, even on Sundays. Such a desired practice was and is simply not physically feasible for parish Priests. But a corps of extraordinary ministers of Holy Communion could, did and continue to do just that.

A 1983 ritual book for the United States, *Pastoral Care of the Sick*, reflects that rapid and enormous development. In its introduction to a chapter on "Communion of the Sick," the text states that Priests with pastoral responsibilities should arrange that the sick or aged, even though not seriously ill or in danger of death, be given opportunities to receive the Eucharist frequently, even daily, especially during Easter Time and particularly on Sundays.

This was not a possibility 50 years ago. Thanks to the introduction of extraordinary ministers of Holy Communion, it is indeed possible and has currently become a common reality in American parishes.

Initial Procedure

THOSE who will for the first time serve as extra-ordinary ministers of Holy Communion to the sick should find the following explanatory steps helpful:

1. A parish Priest or his delegate will identify the who, where and when of the person(s) to receive Communion.

2. The minister needs a special closed vessel in which to carry the host. This could be a metal pyx, a leather container or a cloth burse.

3. The Priest or his delegate will indicate how the Blessed Sacrament host will be obtained,

ideally within Mass, but possibly outside a Eucharistic celebration.

4. The extraordinary minister of Holy Communion, if at all feasible, proceeds directly and without delay to the home of the confined person.

5. Upon arrival, the minister may sit down and visit for a few minutes in a friendly way with the sick person and others who are present.

6. After establishing that cordial rapport, the minister shifts the tone of the experience and begins the Communion ritual. The confined person may have prepared a table with white cloth, candles, crucifix, glass of water and spoon. In most circumstances, however, that will not be the situation. In such instances, the minister merely finds a suitable spot upon which to place the Communion vessel, a location where all can see the pyx, container or burse.

7. The minister follows the ritual provided (pages 9-41). Reading through these texts beforehand will provide a greater familiarity with the prayers and readings as well as afford an opportunity to decide which options will be selected during the actual carrying out of the rite.

8. Afterwards, the minister either returns the vessel to the parish or retains it for future occasion.

9. If this is to become a continual and regular responsibility, the minister will want to study Appendices II and III, "Pastoral Guidelines" and "Inner Qualities" (pp. 45-51).

10. If time and circumstances permit, it might be very fruitful to read the appropriate Gospel to the Communicant. Appendix II, Section 4, *Sacred Scripture*, p. 46, and Appendices V and VI (pp. 54-64) will be helpful in that task.

APPENDIX II
Pastoral Guidelines

E XTRAORDINARY ministers of Holy Communion who carry the Eucharist to those confined at home may find these pastoral suggestions useful.

1. *Official Instructions.* The "Introduction" to the Rite for Communion of the Sick contains in the typically succinct, but profoundly rich style of Church documents many practical, theological and spiritual truths pertinent to this ministry. Those selected for this noble task would do well to read, study and ponder these few pages (pp. 5-7).

2. *Church Community.* A close connection does or should exist between the healthy believers gathered for Mass and those confined persons unable to be present. In addition to prayer for the sick during every Eucharistic celebration, two specific possibilities can underscore this link between those in church and those at home.

a. A Simple Process. The ministers to the sick come forward for Holy Communion with the rest of the community in the usual fashion. However, before their own reception of the host, they open the Communion pyx, container or burse and indicate how many consecrated hosts they need. After placing the filled pyx in their pockets, they receive the Lord themselves and return to their seats, later embarking upon this journey of love to the homebound.

b. A Solemn Process. In this ideal, but not always feasible procedure, the ministers to the sick leave their pyx, containers or burses before Mass with those arranging the liturgy, indicating how many hosts are required. During the distribution of Communion, appropriate persons place the desired numbers in each container and leave these on the altar. Following the Prayer after Communion, the presiding Priest summons the extraordinary ministers of Holy Communion forward and addresses them with these or similar words:

"You special and extraordinary ministers of Holy Communion to the sick, receive the Eucharistic Lord and carry Christ to our beloved homebound parishioners. Tell them we care about and are praying for them. Mention today's message *(here the Priest may summarize the Homily in one or two sentences)*. Ask them to pray for us and to offer their troubles to God on our behalf."

After the dismissal of Mass, they join the altar ministers in the recessional.

3. *Parish connections.* The ministers would do well to pick up a copy or copies of the weekly bulletin and bring these with them to the homebound. In addition, they might tape the Homily or at least make written or mental notes about its major points for use later at the home of those confined. Moreover, thcy also may recall any practical announcements made at the end of the Mass. This information would be communicated after the reading of Scripture and following the Communion service.

4. *Sacred Scripture.* The ritual provides five brief excerpts from the Gospel and the first letter of John. As a praiseworthy alternative to these texts, a minister might bring his or her own Bible and read the Gospel designated for that particular Sunday. Appendix V (pp. 54-59) indicates the correct Sunday for every year through 2029. Appendix VI (pp. 60-64) then identifies the proper Gospel for each Sunday and several major Feasts. A pocket-sized New Testament combined with this ritual booklet should make the task relatively simple and easy.

5. *Universal Prayer.* By paying close attention to the Universal Prayer at Mass, ministers will have some ready-made intentions for the Universal Prayer with the homebound. They, of course, could also create their own petitions and invite further ones from those present. Appendix IV offers guidelines and suggestions for them (pp. 52-53).

6. *Priest's Presence.* Extraordinary ministers of Holy Communion are both desirable and necessary. But occasional or even regular visits by the parish Priest are equally welcome and even essential. Those homebound persons always will gladly receive their shepherd and usually be most grateful for opportunities to receive the Sacraments of Penance and Anointing of the Sick.

7. *Interested Listeners.* Many of the homebound have few occasions to interact with others outside the immediate neighborhood. They thus normally will relish the occasion to visit at length with Communion ministers. Being interested listeners in such situations both fulfills Christ's command to love and greatly comforts those often lonely persons confined at home.

8. *A Healing Touch.* Homebound individuals frequently feel isolated, cut off from the world which surrounds them. A light, gentle touch of hand, brow or head from the extraordinary minister of Holy Communion at some time during the visit helps bridge that gap and makes them feel connected with those outside the home.

9. *Hispanic Homebound.* Because of the ever-increasing number of Hispanic Catholics in North America, this booklet includes the Spanish version of the official ritual for Communion in Ordinary Circumstances and for Communion in a Hospital or Institution.

APPENDIX III

Inner Qualities

THE inner qualities of a person are transparent and translucent. People often simply intuit the interior attitudes, virtues or characteristics of another individual. Those qualities within emerge, surface, become evident to others.

An infant senses when its mother is worried or peaceful, serene or nervous.

Young boys and girls just know that a particular adult truly cares about and loves them. Despite sometimes severe parental and school cautions about such matters, they will spontaneously run up and hug a warm and welcoming older person.

Grown-ups likewise perceive, although not always accurately, inner qualities behind the external manifestations.

Store clerks can project a welcoming, indifferent or even hostile attitude by their mere demeanor.

Those in close relationships understand well that our eyes are the doorways to the soul and that the face aptly communicates feelings. A look can convey love and joy or sorrow and hurt. A face breaks into a smile or a frown.

This truth applies to extraordinary ministers of Holy Communion. Those gathered for worship rather swiftly detect within extraordinary ministers of Holy Communion the presence or absence of certain expected inner qualities. Questions like these may run through their minds:

Do they really believe? Are they prayerful persons? Have they a spirit of awesomeness before the mystery of God and the Eucharist? Do they radiate joy and hospitality? Are they relaxed and unhurried, yet still reverent?

To gain, retain and strengthen such ideal inner qualities is a never-ending task.

1. *Faith.* Faith enables us to look beyond and see something more. Church teachings emphasize that Jesus is present among us in many ways, but especially in the Sacrifice of the Mass and the Eucharistic species. The liturgy is essentially a meeting with Christ in faith. Faith, which may overflow into our feelings, but not necessarily, moves beneath the bread and wine to recognize the Real Presence of the Lord.

"You have faith in God, have faith also in me"(John 14:1).

Read Matthew 15:22-33.

2. *Prayerfulness.* Jesus spent time in personal prayer before important decisions and after significant actions. He also urged the Apostles after their successful preaching and healing efforts to step aside and rest awhile. Over the centuries those who have walked in Christ's footsteps and effectively carried on his ministry have always found regular time for prayerful solitude. A contemporary spiritual writer argues that unless we set aside some time each day for personal prayer, it will be impossible to transform ceaseless activity into a constant awareness of God's presence.

"Come away by yourselves to a deserted place and rest a while"(Mark 6:31).

Read Luke 5:12-16 and 6:12-16.

3. *Awe and wonder.* God ordered Moses to remove his sandals because he was standing on holy ground and before the Almighty One. The prophet Daniel cried out, "Great and awesome God . . . "(Daniel 9:4-10).Those who approached Jesus often did so at a distance and only hesitatingly spoke or reached out to touch him.

"They were filled with awe and amazed and said to one another, 'Who then is this, who commands even the winds and the sea, and they obey him?' " (Luke 8:25).

Read Matthew 2:1-11.

4. *Joy.* Joy is the inevitable sign of the presence of God. That statement, attributed to at least two famous persons, accurately reflects the experience or at least impressions of many over the years. When Mary, carrying Jesus within her, greeted her cousin Elizabeth, also pregnant, the latter observed "that the infant in my womb leaped for joy" (Luke 1:44). The angel announced to the shepherds, "I proclaim to you good news of great joy . . . " (Luke 2:10). When the Risen One appeared to his followers, "The disciples rejoiced . . . " (John 20:20).

Visitors to Trappist monasteries or convents for Mother Teresa of Calcutta's Missionaries of Charity invariably comment afterwards about the joy and happiness reflected in their faces.

"I have told you this so that my joy might be in you and your joy might be complete" (John 15:11).

Read Luke 24:13-35.

5. *Hospitality.* How do Catholics rate the quality of a Sunday liturgy? What criteria are used in such an evaluation?

Surveys indicate that parishioners judge Masses on the basis of these elements: preaching, music, the presiding Priest and hospitality. Persons at the Eucharistic celebrations of model churches feel welcome; worshipers seem to care for each other; parishioners warmly reach out to newcomers or visitors.

The early Christians were one in mind and heart, shared things in common, had no individual in need among them and daily praised God together.

"I was hungry and you gave me food, I was thirsty and you gave me drink, a stranger and you welcomed me . . . " (Matthew 25:35).

Read Acts 2:42-47 and 4:32-35.

6. *Relaxed and unhurried, yet reverent.* The Mass is a sacred meal, a holy banquet. It is a sacred and holy event—we receive the Body and Blood of the Risen Jesus himself. But it is also a meal and banquet, a special supper during which Christ comes to us as he promised and commanded under the signs of bread and wine.

Extraordinary ministers of Holy Communion are obtaining, transporting and distributing to the sick the very Lord Jesus Christ. An awareness of that sublime truth quite naturally will lead to a reverent approach with those tasks.

We try not to rush through elegant banquets, formal dinners or even a main family meal. Participation by the ill or homebound through Communion in this unique Eucharistic supper warrants a similar unhurried pace. Moreover, that slower style of service conveys a willingness on the part of ministers to stay and visit, rather than an obvious anxiety to finish and leave.

Since Jesus gave himself to us in the Eucharist for eating and drinking, we have to expect that crumbs will fall and, at Mass, wine will spill. So, too, on occasions extraordinary ministers of Holy Communion may drop the host, find Communicants experience difficulty consuming the Lord's Body or wonder if seriously ill persons are fully conscious of what is happening. In such situations they need to remain peaceful, relaxed and comfortable, even while ministering with the reverence called for by their ministry.

"They picked up the fragments left over—seven baskets full" (Matthew 15:37).

Read 1 Corinthians 11:23-29.

APPENDIX IV

Universal Prayer

WE have become familiar over the past quarter of a century with the Universal Prayer or Prayer of the Faithful. As a result of decisions at the Second Vatican Council, the revised Roman Missal in 1969 resurrected this ancient formula, inserting it after the Creed or homily. In it, the people or faithful intercede for or pray for all humankind.

These petitions in general are for the Church, civil authorities, those oppressed by various needs, for all humankind and for the salvation of the world.

Normally, the petitions follow this sequence:
—For needs of the Church.
—For public authorities and the salvation of the world.
—For those oppressed by any need.
—For the local community.

On special occasions, e.g., Thanksgiving, the Nativity of the Lord, Lent, Easter, summer time, a petition or petitions usually will reflect that season or situation.

As we have noted, by listening carefully to those announced at weekend Mass, the minister will have at hand some current intercessions to use.

There are a variety of available responses. "Lord, receive our prayer" is more suitable than "Lord, hear our prayer" or "Lord, hear us." The latter two pose difficult challenges for those persons with impaired hearing.

The following is a sample Universal Prayer or Prayer of the Faithful:

The response is: "Lord, receive our prayer."

For our Holy Father, the Pope, that the Holy Spirit will give him wisdom and strength, we pray to the Lord.

For our President and all leaders of government, that they may be effective in eliminating poverty and achieving peace, we pray to the Lord.

For our young people, that they may use their talents well for building up the Church and making this a better world, we pray to the Lord.

For those who are ill, that they may be comforted and strengthened by Christ's presence, we pray to the Lord.

For those who have died, that they may now see the Lord face-to-face, we pray to the Lord.

Any intentions you would like to pray for? . . .

All-powerful and loving God, you are close to the brokenhearted and near to those crushed in spirit; grant these petitions which with faith we present to you through Christ our Lord. Amen.

APPENDIX V

Calendar of Sundays

YEAR A

Sunday or Feast	2013	2016	2019	2022	2025	2028
1st Sunday of Advent	Dec. 1	Nov. 27	Dec. 1	Nov. 27	Nov. 30	Dec. 3
Immaculate Conception	—	Dec. 8.	—	Dec. 8	Dec. 8	Dec. 8
2nd Sunday of Advent	Dec. 8	Dec. 4	Dec. 8	Dec. 4	Dec. 7	Dec. 10
3rd Sunday of Advent	Dec. 15	Dec. 11	Dec. 15	Dec. 11	Dec. 14	Dec. 17
4th Sunday of Advent	Dec. 22	Dec. 18	Dec. 22	Dec. 18	Dec. 21	Dec. 24
Nativity of the Lord	Dec. 25	Dec. 25	Dec. 25	Dec. 25	Dec. 25	Dec. 25
Holy Family	Dec. 29	—	Dec. 29	—	Dec. 28	Dec. 31

Sunday or Feast	2014	2017	2020	2023	2026	2029
Mary, the Holy Mother of God	Jan. 1	Jan. 1	Jan. 1	Jan. 1	Jan. 1	Jan. 1
Epiphany of the Lord	Jan. 5	Jan. 8	Jan. 5	Jan. 8	Jan. 4	Jan. 7
Baptism of the Lord	Jan. 12	—	Jan. 12	—	Jan. 11	—
2nd Sunday in Ordinary Time	Jan. 19	Jan. 15	Jan. 19	Jan. 15	Jan. 18	Jan. 14
3rd Sunday in Ordinary Time	Jan. 26	Jan. 22	Jan. 26	Jan. 22	Jan. 25	Jan. 21
4th Sunday in Ordinary Time	Feb. 2	Jan. 29	Feb. 2	Jan. 29	Feb. 1	Jan. 28
5th Sunday in Ordinary Time	Feb. 9	Feb. 5	Feb. 9	Feb. 5	Feb. 8	Feb. 4
6th Sunday in Ordinary Time	Feb. 16	Feb. 12	Feb. 16	Feb. 12	Feb. 15	Feb. 11
7th Sunday in Ordinary Time	Feb. 23	Feb. 19	Feb. 23	Feb. 19	—	—
8th Sunday in Ordinary Time	Mar. 2	Feb. 26	—	—	—	—
9th Sunday in Ordinary Time	—	—	—	—	—	—
1st Sunday of Lent	Mar. 9	Mar. 5	Mar. 1	Feb. 26	Feb. 22	Feb. 18
2nd Sunday of Lent	Mar. 16	Mar. 12	Mar. 8	Mar. 5	Mar. 1	Feb. 25
3rd Sunday of Lent	Mar. 23	Mar. 19	Mar. 15	Mar. 12	Mar. 8	Mar. 4
4th Sunday of Lent	Mar. 30	Mar. 26	Mar. 22	Mar. 19	Mar. 15	Mar. 11
5th Sunday of Lent	Apr. 6	Apr. 2	Mar. 29	Mar. 26	Mar. 22	Mar. 18
Palm Sunday	Apr. 13	Apr. 9	Apr. 5	Apr. 2	Mar. 29	Mar. 25
Holy Thursday, Chrism Mass	Apr. 17	Apr. 13	Apr. 9	Apr. 6	Apr. 2	Mar. 29
Holy Thursday, Lord's Supper	Apr. 17	Apr. 13	Apr. 9	Apr. 6	Apr. 2	Mar. 29
Good Friday	Apr. 18	Apr. 14	Apr. 10	Apr. 7	Apr. 3	Mar. 30
Easter Vigil	Apr. 19	Apr. 15	Apr. 11	Apr. 8	Apr. 4	Mar. 31
Easter Sunday	Apr. 20	Apr. 16	Apr. 12	Apr. 9	Apr. 5	Apr. 1
2nd Sunday of Easter	Apr. 27	Apr. 23	Apr. 19	Apr. 16	Apr. 12	Apr. 8
3rd Sunday of Easter	May 4	Apr. 30	Apr. 26	Apr. 23	Apr. 19	Apr. 15
4th Sunday of Easter	May 11	May 7	May 3	Apr. 30	Apr. 26	Apr. 22
5th Sunday of Easter	May 18	May 14	May 10	May 7	May 3	Apr. 29

On the dates in red, readings as indicated on p. 64.

YEAR A

Sunday or Feast	2014	2017	2020	2023	2026	2029
6th Sunday of Easter	May 25	May 21	May 17	May 14	May 10	May 6
Ascension of the Lord	May 29	May 25	May 21	May 18	May 14	May 10
7th Sunday of Easter	June 1	May 28	May 24	May 21	May 17	May 13
Pentecost Sunday	June 8	June 4	May 31	May 28	May 24	May 20
Most Holy Trinity	June 15	June 11	June 7	June 4	May 31	May 27
Most Holy Body & Blood	June 22	June 18	June 14	June 11	June 7	June 3
9th Sunday in Ordinary Time	—	—	—	—	—	—
10th Sunday in Ordinary Time	—	—	—	—	—	June 10
11th Sunday in Ordinary Time	—	—	—	June 18	June 14	June 17
12th Sunday in Ordinary Time	—	June 25	June 21	June 25	June 21	June 24
13th Sunday in Ordinary Time	June 29	July 2	June 28	July 2	June 28	July 1
14th Sunday in Ordinary Time	July 6	July 9	July 5	July 9	July 5	July 8
15th Sunday in Ordinary Time	July 13	July 16	July 12	July 16	July 12	July 15
16th Sunday in Ordinary Time	July 20	July 23	July 19	July 23	July 19	July 22
17th Sunday in Ordinary Time	July 27	July 30	July 26	July 30	July 26	July 29
18th Sunday in Ordinary Time	Aug. 3	Aug. 6	Aug. 2	Aug. 6	Aug. 2	Aug. 5
19th Sunday in Ordinary Time	Aug. 10	Aug. 13	Aug. 9	Aug. 13	Aug. 9	Aug. 12
Assumption of the BVM	Aug. 15	Aug. 15	Aug. 15	Aug. 15	Aug. 15	Aug. 15
20th Sunday in Ordinary Time	Aug. 17	Aug. 20	Aug. 16	Aug. 20	Aug. 16	Aug. 19
21st Sunday in Ordinary Time	Aug. 24	Aug. 27	Aug. 23	Aug. 27	Aug. 23	Aug. 26
22nd Sunday in Ordinary Time	Aug. 31	Sept. 3	Aug. 30	Sept. 3	Aug. 30	Sept. 2
23rd Sunday in Ordinary Time	Sept. 7	Sept. 10	Sept. 6	Sept. 10	Sept. 6	Sept. 9
24th Sunday in Ordinary Time	Sept. 14	Sept. 17	Sept. 13	Sept. 17	Sept. 13	Sept. 16
25th Sunday in Ordinary Time	Sept. 21	Sept. 24	Sept. 20	Sept. 24	Sept. 20	Sept. 23
26th Sunday in Ordinary Time	Sept. 28	Oct. 1	Sept. 27	Oct. 1	Sept. 27	Sept. 30
27th Sunday in Ordinary Time	Oct. 5	Oct. 8	Oct. 4	Oct. 8	Oct. 4	Oct. 7
28th Sunday in Ordinary Time	Oct. 12	Oct. 15	Oct. 11	Oct. 15	Oct. 11	Oct. 14
29th Sunday in Ordinary Time	Oct. 19	Oct. 22	Oct 18	Oct. 22	Oct. 18	Oct. 21
30th Sunday in Ordinary Time	Oct. 26	Oct. 29	Oct. 25	Oct. 29	Oct. 25	Oct. 28
All Saints	Nov. 1	Nov. 1	Nov. 1	Nov. 1	Nov. 1	Nov. 1
31st Sunday in Ordinary Time	Nov. 2	Nov. 5	—	Nov. 5	—	Nov. 4
32nd Sunday in Ordinary Time	Nov. 9	Nov. 12	Nov. 8	Nov. 12	Nov. 8	Nov. 11
33rd Sunday in Ordinary Time	Nov. 16	Nov. 19	Nov. 15	Nov. 19	Nov. 15	Nov. 18
Christ, King of the Universe	Nov. 23	Nov. 26	Nov. 22	Nov. 26	Nov. 22	Nov. 25

YEAR B

Sunday or Feast	2011	2014	2017	2020	2023	2026
1st Sunday of Advent	Nov. 27	Nov. 30	Dec. 3	Nov. 29	Dec. 3	Nov. 29
Immaculate Conception	Dec. 8	Dec. 8	Dec. 8	Dec. 8	Dec. 8	Dec. 8
2nd Sunday of Advent	Dec. 4	Dec. 7	Dec. 10	Dec. 6	Dec. 10	Dec. 6
3rd Sunday of Advent	Dec. 11	Dec. 14	Dec. 17	Dec. 13	Dec. 17	Dec. 13
4th Sunday of Advent	Dec. 18	Dec. 21	Dec. 24	Dec. 20	Dec. 24	Dec. 20
Nativity of the Lord	Dec. 25	Dec. 25	Dec. 25	Dec. 25	Dec. 25	Dec. 25
Holy Family	—	28 Dec.	Dec. 31	Dec. 27	Dec. 31	Dec. 27

Sunday or Feast	2012	2015	2018	2021	2024	2027
Mary, the Holy Mother of God	Jan. 1	Jan. 1	Jan. 1	Jan. 1	Jan. 1	Jan. 1
Epiphany of the Lord	Jan. 8	Jan. 4	Jan. 7	Jan. 3	Jan. 7	Jan. 3
Baptism of the Lord	—	Jan. 11	—	Jan. 10	—	Jan. 10
2nd Sunday in Ordinary Time	Jan. 15	Jan. 18	Jan. 14	Jan. 17	Jan. 14	Jan. 17
3rd Sunday in Ordinary Time	Jan. 22	Jan. 25	Jan. 21	Jan. 24	Jan. 21	Jan. 24
4th Sunday in Ordinary Time	Jan. 29	Feb. 1	Jan. 28	Jan. 31	Jan. 28	Jan. 31
5th Sunday in Ordinary Time	Feb. 5	Feb. 8	Feb. 4	Feb. 7	Feb. 4	Feb. 7
6th Sunday in Ordinary Time	Feb. 12	Feb. 15	Feb. 11	Feb. 14	Feb. 11	—
7th Sunday in Ordinary Time	Feb. 19	—	—	—	—	—
8th Sunday in Ordinary Time	—	—	—	—	—	—
9th Sunday in Ordinary Time	—	—	—	—	—	—
1st Sunday of Lent	Feb. 26	Feb. 22	Feb. 18	Feb. 21	Feb. 18	Feb. 14
2nd Sunday of Lent	Mar. 4	Mar. 1	Feb. 25	Feb. 28	Feb. 25	Feb. 21
3rd Sunday of Lent	Mar. 11	Mar. 8	Mar. 4	Mar. 7	Mar. 3	Feb. 28
4th Sunday of Lent	Mar. 18	Mar. 15	Mar. 11	Mar. 14	Mar. 10	Mar. 7
5th Sunday of Lent	Mar. 25	Mar. 22	Mar. 18	Mar. 21	Mar. 17	Mar. 14
Palm Sunday	Apr. 1	Mar. 29	Mar. 25	Mar. 28	Mar. 24	Mar. 21
Holy Thursday, Chrism Mass	Apr. 5	Apr. 2	Mar. 29	Apr. 1	Mar. 28	Mar. 25
Holy Thursday, Lord's Supper	Apr. 5	Apr. 2	Mar. 29	Apr. 1	Mar. 28	Mar. 25
Good Friday	Apr. 6	Apr. 3	Mar. 30	Apr. 2	Mar. 29	Mar. 26
Easter Vigil	Apr. 7	Apr. 4	Mar. 31	Apr. 3	Mar. 30	Mar. 27
Easter Sunday	Apr. 8	Apr. 5	Apr. 1	Apr. 4	Mar. 31	Mar. 28
2nd Sunday of Easter	Apr. 15	Apr. 12	Apr. 8	Apr. 11	Apr. 7	Apr. 4
3rd Sunday of Easter	Apr. 22	Apr. 19	Apr. 15	Apr. 18	Apr. 14	Apr. 11
4th Sunday of Easter	Apr. 29	Apr. 26	Apr. 22	Apr. 25	Apr. 21	Apr. 18
5th Sunday of Easter	May 6	May 3	Apr. 29	May 2	Apr. 28	Apr. 25

On the dates in red, readings as indicated on p. 64.

YEAR B

Sunday or Feast	2012	2015	2018	2021	2024	2027
6th Sunday of Easter	May 13	May 10	May 6	May 9	May 5	May 2
Ascension of the Lord	May 17	May 14	May 10	May 13	May 9	May 6
7th Sunday of Easter	May 20	May 17	May 13	May 16	May 12	May 9
Pentecost Sunday	May 27	May 24	May 20	May 23	May 19	May 16
Most Holy Trinity	June 3	May 31	May 27	May 30	May 26	May 23
Most Holy Body & Blood	June 10	June 7	June 3	June 6	June 2	May 30
9th Sunday in Ordinary Time	—	—	—	—	—	—
10th Sunday in Ordinary Time	—	—	June 10	—	June 9	June 6
11th Sunday in Ordinary Time	June 17	June 14	June 17	June 13	June 16	June 13
12th Sunday in Ordinary Time	June 24	June 21	June 24	June 20	June 23	June 20
13th Sunday in Ordinary Time	July 1	June 28	July 1	June 27	June 30	June 27
14th Sunday in Ordinary Time	July 8	July 5	July 8	July 4	July 7	July 4
15th Sunday in Ordinary Time	July 15	July 12	July 15	July 11	July 14	July 11
16th Sunday in Ordinary Time	July 22	July 19	July 22	July 18	July 21	July 18
17th Sunday in Ordinary Time	July 29	July 26	July 29	July 25	July 28	July 25
18th Sunday in Ordinary Time	Aug. 5	Aug. 2	Aug. 5	Aug. 1	Aug. 4	Aug. 1
19th Sunday in Ordinary Time	Aug. 12	Aug. 9	Aug. 12	Aug. 8	Aug. 11	Aug. 8
Assumption of the BVM	Aug. 15	Aug. 15	Aug. 15	Aug. 15	Aug. 15	Aug. 15
20th Sunday in Ordinary Time	Aug. 19	Aug. 16	Aug. 19	—	Aug. 18	—
21st Sunday in Ordinary Time	Aug. 26	Aug. 23	Aug. 26	Aug. 22	Aug. 25	Aug. 22
22nd Sunday in Ordinary Time	Sept. 2	Aug. 30	Sept. 2	Aug. 29	Sept. 1	Aug. 29
23rd Sunday in Ordinary Time	Sept. 9	Sept. 6	Sept. 9	Sept. 5	Sept. 8	Sept. 5
24th Sunday in Ordinary Time	Sept. 16	Sept. 13	Sept. 16	Sept. 12	Sept. 15	Sept. 12
25th Sunday in Ordinary Time	Sept. 23	Sept. 20	Sept. 23	Sept. 19	Sept. 22	Sept. 19
26th Sunday in Ordinary Time	Sept. 30	Sept. 27	Sept. 30	Sept. 26	Sept. 29	Sept. 26
27th Sunday in Ordinary Time	Oct. 7	Oct. 4	Oct. 7	Oct. 3	Oct. 6	Oct. 3
28th Sunday in Ordinary Time	Oct. 14	Oct. 11	Oct. 14	Oct. 10	Oct. 13	Oct. 10
29th Sunday in Ordinary Time	Oct. 21	Oct. 18	Oct. 21	Oct. 17	Oct. 20	Oct. 17
30th Sunday in Ordinary Time	Oct. 28	Oct. 25	Oct 28	Oct. 24	Oct. 27	Oct. 24
All Saints	Nov. 1	Nov. 1	Nov. 1	Nov. 1	Nov. 1	Nov. 1
31st Sunday in Ordinary Time	Nov. 4	—	Nov. 4	Oct. 31	Nov. 3	Oct. 31
32nd Sunday in Ordinary Time	Nov. 11	Nov. 8	Nov. 11	Nov. 7	Nov. 10	Nov. 7
33rd Sunday in Ordinary Time	Nov. 18	Nov. 15	Nov. 18	Nov. 14	Nov. 17	Nov. 14
Christ, King of the Universe	Nov. 25	Nov. 22	Nov. 25	Nov. 21	Nov. 24	Nov. 21

YEAR C

Sunday or Feast	2012	2015	2018	2021	2024	2027
1st Sunday of Advent	Dec. 2	Nov. 29	Dec. 2	Nov. 28	Dec. 1	Nov. 28
Immaculate Conception	Dec. 8	Dec. 8	Dec. 8	Dec. 8	—	Dec. 8
2nd Sunday of Advent	Dec. 9	Dec. 6	Dec. 9	Dec. 5	Dec. 8	Dec. 5
3rd Sunday of Advent	Dec.16	Dec. 13	Dec. 16	Dec. 12	Dec. 15	Dec. 12
4th Sunday of Advent	Dec. 23	Dec. 20	Dec. 23	Dec. 19	Dec. 22	Dec. 19
Nativity of the Lord	Dec. 25	Dec. 25	Dec. 25	Dec. 25	Dec. 25	Dec. 25
Holy Family	Dec. 30	Dec. 27	Dec 30	Dec. 26	Dec. 29	Dec. 26
Sunday or Feast	**2013**	**2016**	**2019**	**2022**	**2025**	**2028**
Mary, the Holy Mother of God	Jan. 1	Jan. 1	Jan. 1	Jan. 1	Jan. 1	Jan. 1
Epiphany of the Lord	Jan. 6	Jan. 3	Jan. 6	Jan. 2	Jan. 5	Jan. 2
Baptism of the Lord	Jan. 13	Jan. 10	Jan. 13	Jan. 9	Jan. 12	Jan. 9
2nd Sunday in Ordinary Time	Jan. 20	Jan. 17	Jan. 20	Jan. 16	Jan. 19	Jan. 16
3rd Sunday in Ordinary Time	Jan. 27	Jan. 24	Jan. 27	Jan. 23	Jan. 26	Jan. 23
4th Sunday in Ordinary Time	Feb. 3	Jan. 31	Feb. 3	Jan. 30	Feb. 2	Jan. 30
5th Sunday in Ordinary Time	Feb. 10	Feb. 7	Feb 10	Feb. 6	Feb. 9	Feb. 6
6th Sunday in Ordinary Time	—	—	Feb. 17	Feb. 13	Feb. 16	Feb. 13
7th Sunday in Ordinary Time	—	—	Feb. 24	Feb. 20	Feb. 23	Feb. 20
8th Sunday in Ordinary Time	—	—	Mar. 3	Feb. 27	Mar. 2	Feb. 27
9th Sunday in Ordinary Time	—	—	—	—	—	—
1st Sunday of Lent	Feb. 17	Feb. 14	Mar. 10	Mar. 6	Mar. 9	Mar. 5
2nd Sunday of Lent	Feb. 24	Feb. 21	Mar. 17	Mar. 13	Mar. 16	Mar. 12
3rd Sunday of Lent	Mar. 3	Feb. 28	Mar. 24	Mar. 20	Mar. 23	Mar. 19
4th Sunday of Lent	Mar. 10	Mar. 6	Mar. 31	Mar. 27	Mar. 30	Mar. 26
5th Sunday of Lent	Mar. 17	Mar. 13	Apr. 7	Apr. 3	Apr. 6	Apr. 2
Palm Sunday	Mar. 24	Mar. 20	Apr. 14	Apr. 10	Apr. 13	Apr. 9
Holy Thursday, Chrism Mass	Mar. 28	Mar. 24	Apr 18	Apr. 14	Apr. 17	Apr. 13
Holy Thursday, Lord's Supper	Mar. 28	Mar. 24	Apr. 18	Apr. 14	Apr. 17	Apr. 13
Good Friday	Mar. 29	Mar. 25	Apr. 19	Apr. 15	Apr. 18	Apr. 14
Easter Vigil	Mar. 30	Mar. 26	Apr. 20	Apr. 16	Apr. 19	Apr. 15
Easter Sunday	Mar. 31	Mar. 27	Apr. 21	Apr. 17	Apr. 20	Apr. 16
2nd Sunday of Easter	Apr. 7	Apr. 3	Apr. 28	Apr. 24	Apr. 27	Apr. 23
3rd Sunday of Easter	Apr. 14	Apr. 10	May 5	May 1	May 4	Apr. 30
4th Sunday of Easter	Apr. 21	Apr. 17	May 12	May 8	May 11	May 7
5th Sunday of Easter	Apr. 28	Apr. 24	May 19	May 15	May 18	May 14

On the dates in red, readings as indicated on p. 64.

YEAR C

Sunday or Feast	2013	2016	2019	2022	2025	2028
6th Sunday of Easter	May 5	May 1	May 26	May 22	May 25	May 21
Ascension of the Lord	May 9	May 5	May 30	May 26	May 29	May 25
7th Sunday of Easter	May 12	May 8	June 2	May 29	June 1	May 28
Pentecost Sunday	May 19	May 15	June 9	June 5	June 8	June 4
Most Holy Trinity	May 26	May 22	June 16	June 12	June 15	June 11
Most Holy Body & Blood	June 2	May 29	June 23	June 19	June 22	June 18
9th Sunday in Ordinary Time	—	—	—	—	—	—
10th Sunday in Ordinary Time	June 9	June 5	—	—	—	—
11th Sunday in Ordinary Time	June 16	June 12	—	—	—	—
12th Sunday in Ordinary Time	June 23	June 19	—	—	—	June 25
13th Sunday in Ordinary Time	June 30	June 26	June 30	June 26	June 29	July 2
14th Sunday in Ordinary Time	July 7	July 3	July 7	July 3	July 6	July 9
15th Sunday in Ordinary Time	July 14	July 10	July 14	July 10	July 13	July 16
16th Sunday in Ordinary Time	July 21	July 17	July 21	July 17	July 20	July 23
17th Sunday in Ordinary Time	July 28	July 24	July 28	July 24	July 27	July 30
18th Sunday in Ordinary Time	Aug. 4	July 31	Aug. 4	July 31	Aug. 3	Aug. 6
19th Sunday in Ordinary Time	Aug. 11	Aug. 7	Aug. 11	Aug. 7	Aug. 10	Aug. 13
Assumption of the BVM	Aug. 15	Aug. 15	Aug. 15	Aug. 15	Aug. 15	Aug. 15
20th Sunday in Ordinary Time	Aug. 18	Aug. 14	Aug. 18	Aug. 14	Aug. 17	Aug. 20
21st Sunday in Ordinary Time	Aug. 25	Aug. 21	Aug. 25	Aug. 21	Aug. 24	Aug. 27
22nd Sunday in Ordinary Time	Sept. 1	Aug. 28	Sept. 1	Aug. 28	Aug. 31	Sept. 3
23rd Sunday in Ordinary Time	Sept. 8	Sept. 4	Sept. 8	Sept. 4	Sept. 7	Sept. 10
24th Sunday in Ordinary Time	Sept. 15	Sept. 11	Sept. 15	Sept. 11	Sept. 14	Sept. 17
25th Sunday in Ordinary Time	Sept. 22	Sept. 18	Sept. 22	Sept. 18	Sept. 21	Sept. 24
26th Sunday in Ordinary Time	Sept. 29	Sept. 25	Sept. 29	Sept. 25	Sept. 28	Oct. 1
27th Sunday in Ordinary Time	Oct. 6	Oct. 2	Oct. 6	Oct. 2	Oct. 5	Oct. 8
28th Sunday in Ordinary Time	Oct. 13	Oct. 9	Oct. 13	Oct. 9	Oct. 12	Oct. 15
29th Sunday in Ordinary Time	Oct. 20	Oct. 16	Oct. 20	Oct. 16	Oct. 19	Oct. 22
30th Sunday in Ordinary Time	Oct. 27	Oct. 23	Oct. 27	Oct. 23	Oct. 26	Oct. 29
All Saints	Nov. 1	Nov. 1	Nov. 1	Nov. 1	Nov. 1	Nov. 1
31st Sunday in Ordinary Time	Nov. 3	Oct. 30	Nov. 3	Oct. 30	Nov. 2	Nov. 5
32nd Sunday in Ordinary Time	Nov. 10	Nov. 6	Nov. 10	Nov. 6	Nov. 9	Nov. 12
33rd Sunday in Ordinary Time	Nov. 17	Nov. 13	Nov. 17	Nov. 13	Nov. 16	Nov. 19
Christ, King of the Universe	Nov. 24	Nov. 20	Nov. 24	Nov. 20	Nov. 23	Nov. 26

APPENDIX VI

List of the Sunday Gospels

YEAR A

ADVENT

1st Sunday of Advent—Mt 24:37-44
2nd Sunday of Advent—Mt 3:1-12
3rd Sunday of Advent—Mt 11:2-11
4th Sunday of Advent—Mt 1:18-24

CHRISTMAS TIME

Nativity of the Lord [Christmas]
  (Vigil)—Mt 1:1-25
(Mass during the Night)—Lk 2:1-14
(Mass at Dawn)—Lk 2:15-20
(Mass during the Day)—Jn 1:1-18
Sunday after the Nativity [Christmas]
  (Holy Family)—Mt 2:13-15, 19-23
January 1 (Solemnity of Mary, the
  Holy Mother of God)—Lk 2:16-21
2nd Sunday after the Nativity
  [Christmas]—Jn 1:1-18
Epiphany of the Lord (Vigil and
  During the Day)—Mt 2:1-12
Sunday after Epiphany (Baptism
  of the Lord)—Mt 3:13-17

LENT

Ash Wednesday—Mt 6:1-6, 16-18
1st Sunday of Lent—Mt 4:1-11
2nd Sunday of Lent—Mt 17:1-9
3rd Sunday of Lent—Jn 4:5-42
4th Sunday of Lent—Jn 9:1-41
5th Sunday of Lent—Jn 11:1-45
Palm Sunday of the Passion of the
  Lord
  —Procession: Mt 21:1-11
  —Mt 26:14—27:66

Holy Thursday Chrism Mass
  —Lk 4:16-21

SACRED PASCHAL TRIDUUM AND EASTER TIME

Mass of the Lord's Supper—
  Jn 13:1-15
Good Friday—Jn 18:1—19:42
Easter Vigil—Mt 28:1-10
Easter Sunday—Jn 20:1-9
  or Mt 28:1-10
  Evening: Lk 24:13-35
2nd Sunday of Easter—Jn 20:19-31
3rd Sunday of Easter—Lk 24:13-35
4th Sunday of Easter—Jn 10:1-10
5th Sunday of Easter—Jn 14:1-12
6th Sunday of Easter—Jn 14:15-21
Ascension of the Lord (Vigil and
  During the Day)—Mt 28:16-20
7th Sunday of Easter—Jn 17:1-11a
Pentecost (Vigil)—Jn 7:37-39
(Mass during the Day)—Jn 20:19-23

SOLEMNITIES OF THE LORD DURING ORDINARY TIME

Most Holy Trinity (Sunday after
  Pentecost)—Jn 3:16-18
Most Holy Body and Blood of
  Christ—Jn 6:51-58
Most Sacred Heart of Jesus—
  Mt 11:25-30

ORDINARY TIME

1st Sunday—See Baptism of
  the Lord, above

2nd Sunday—Jn 1:29-34
3rd Sunday—Mt 4:12-23
4th Sunday—Mt 5:1-12a
5th Sunday—Mt 5:13-16
6th Sunday—Mt 5:17-37
7th Sunday—Mt 5:38-48
8th Sunday—Mt 6:24-34
9th Sunday—Mt 7:21-27
10th Sunday—Mt 9:9-13
11th Sunday—Mt 9:36—10:8
12th Sunday—Mt 10:26-33
13th Sunday—Mt 10:37-42
14th Sunday—Mt 11:25-30
15th Sunday—Mt 13:1-23
16th Sunday—Mt 13:24-43
17th Sunday—Mt 13:44-52
18th Sunday—Mt 14:13-21

19th Sunday—Mt 14:22-33
20th Sunday—Mt 15:21-28
21st Sunday—Mt 16:13-20
22nd Sunday—Mt 16:21-27
23rd Sunday—Mt 18:15-20
24th Sunday—Mt 18:21-35
25th Sunday—Mt 20:1-16a
26th Sunday—Mt 21:28-32
27th Thursday—Mt 21:33-43
28th Sunday—Mt 22:1-14
29th Sunday—Mt 22:15-21
30th Sunday—Mt 22:34-40
31st Sunday—Mt 23:1-12
32nd Sunday—Mt 25:1-13
33rd Sunday—Mt 25:14-30
34th Sunday (Our Lord Jesus Christ,
    King of the Universe)—
    Mt 25:31-46

YEAR B

ADVENT

1st Sunday of Advent—Mk 13:33-37
2nd Sunday of Advent—Mk 1:1-8
3rd Sunday of Advent—
    Jn 1:6-8, 19-28
4th Sunday of Advent—Lk 1:26-38

CHRISTMAS TIME

Nativity of the Lord [Christmas]
    (Vigil)—Mt 1:1-25
(Mass during the Night)—Lk 2:1-14
(Mass at Dawn)—Lk 2:15-20
(Mass during the Day)—Jn 1:1-18
Sunday after the Nativity [Christmas]
    (Holy Family)—Lk 2:22-40
January 1 (Solemnity of Mary, the
    Holy Mother of God)—Lk 2:16-21
2nd Sunday after the Nativity
    [Christmas]—Jn 1:1-18
Epiphany of the Lord (Vigil and
    During the Day)—Mt 2:1-12

Sunday after Epiphany (Baptism
    of the Lord)—Mk 1:7-11

LENT

Ash Wednesday—Mt 6:1-6, 16-18
1st Sunday of Lent—Mk 1:12-15
2nd Sunday of Lent—Mk 9:2-10
3rd Sunday of Lent—Jn 2:13-25
4th Sunday of Lent—Jn 3:14-21
5th Sunday of Lent—Jn 12:20-33
Palm Sunday of the Passion of the
    Lord
    —Procession: Mk 11:1-10
    or Jn 12:12-16
    —Mk 14:1—15:47
Holy Thursday Chrism Mass
    —Lk 4:16-21

SACRED PASCHAL TRIDUUM AND EASTER TIME

Mass of the Lord's Supper—
    Jn 13:1-15

Good Friday—Jn 18:1—19:42
Easter Vigil—Mk 16:1-7
Easter Sunday—Jn 20:1-9
   or Mk 16:1-7
   Evening: Lk 24:13-35
2nd Sunday of Easter—Jn 20:19-31
3rd Sunday of Easter—Lk 24:35-48
4th Sunday of Easter—Jn 10:11-18
5th Sunday of Easter—Jn 15:1-8
6th Sunday of Easter—Jn 15:9-17
Ascension of the Lord (Vigil and
   During the Day)—Mk 16:15-20
7th Sunday of Easter—
   Jn 17:11b-19
Pentecost (Vigil)—Jn 7:37-39
(Mass during the Day)—Jn 20:19-23
   or Jn 15:26-27; 16:12-15

SOLEMNITIES OF THE LORD DURING ORDINARY TIME

Most Holy Trinity (Sunday after
   Pentecost)—Mt 28:16-20
Most Holy Body and Blood of
   Christ—Mt 14:12-16, 22-26
Most Sacred Heart of Jesus—
   Jn 19:31-37

ORDINARY TIME

1st Sunday—See Baptism of
   the Lord, above
2nd Sunday—Jn 1:35-42
3rd Sunday—Mk 1:14-20
4th Sunday—Mk 1:21-28
5th Sunday—Mk 1:29-39
6th Sunday—Mk 1:40-45
7th Sunday—Mk 2:1-12
8th Sunday—Mk 2:18-22
9th Sunday—Mk 2:23—3:6
10th Sunday—Mk 3:20-35
11th Sunday—Mk 4:26-34
12th Sunday—Mk 4:35-41
13th Sunday—Mk 5:21-43
14th Sunday—Mk 6:1-6
15th Sunday—Mk 6:7-13
16th Sunday—Mk 6:30-34
17th Sunday—Jn 6:1-15
18th Sunday—Jn 6:24-35
19th Sunday—Jn 6:41-51
20th Sunday—Jn 6:51-58
21st Sunday—Jn 6:60-69
22nd Sunday—Mk 7:1-8, 14-15,
   21-23
23rd Sunday—Mk 7:31-37
24th Sunday—Mk 8:27-35
25th Sunday—Mk 9:30-37
26th Sunday—Mk 9:38-43, 45,
   47-48
27th Sunday—Mk 10:2-16
28th Sunday—Mk 10:17-30
29th Sunday—Mk 10:35-45
30th Sunday—Mk 10:46-52
31st Sunday—Mk 12:28b-34
32nd Sunday—Mk 12:38-44
33rd Sunday—Mk 13:24-32
34th Sunday (Our Lord Jesus Christ,
   King of the Universe)—
   Jn 18:33b-37

YEAR C

ADVENT

1st Sunday of Advent—Lk 21:25-28, 34-36

2nd Sunday of Advent—Lk 3:1-6

3rd Sunday of Advent—Lk 3:10-18

4th Sunday of Advent—Lk 1:39-45

CHRISTMAS TIME

Nativity of the Lord [Christmas] (Vigil)—Mt 1:1-25

(Mass during the Night)—Lk 2:1-14

(Mass at Dawn)—Lk 2:15-20

(Mass during the Day)—Jn 1:1-18

Sunday after the Nativity [Christmas] (Holy Family)—Lk 2:41-52

January 1 (Solemnity of Mary, the Holy Mother of God)—Lk 2:16-21

2nd Sunday after the Nativity [Christmas]—Jn 1:1-18

Epiphany of the Lord (Vigil and During the Day)—Mt 2:1-12

Sunday after Epiphany (Baptism of the Lord)—Lk 3:15-16, 21-22

LENT

Ash Wednesday—Mt 6:1-6, 16-18

1st Sunday of Lent—Lk 4:1-13

2nd Sunday of Lent—Lk 9:28b-36

3rd Sunday of Lent—Lk 13:1-9

4th Sunday of Lent—Lk 15:1-3, 11-32

5th Sunday of Lent—Jn 8:1-11

Palm Sunday of the Passion of the Lord

—Procession: Lk 19:28-40

—Lk 22:14—23:56

Holy Thursday Chrism Mass —Lk 4:16-21

SACRED PASCHAL TRIDUUM AND EASTER TIME

Mass of the Lord's Supper—Jn 13:1-15

Good Friday—Jn 18:1—19:42

Easter Vigil—Lk 24:1-12

Easter Sunday—Jn 20:1-9 or Lk 24:1-12 Evening: Lk 24:13-35

2nd Sunday of Easter—Jn 20:19-31

3rd Sunday of Easter—Jn 21:1-19

4th Sunday of Easter—Jn 10:27-30

5th Sunday of Easter— Jn 13:31-33a, 34-35

6th Sunday of Easter—Jn 14:23-29

Ascension of the Lord (Vigil and During the Day)—Lk 24:46-53

7th Sunday of Easter—Jn 17:20-26

Pentecost (Vigil)—Jn 7:37-39

(Mass during the Day)—Jn 20:19-23 or Jn 14:15-16, 23b-26

SOLEMNITIES OF THE LORD DURING ORDINARY TIME

Most Holy Trinity (Sunday after Pentecost)—Jn 16:12-15

Most Holy Body and Blood of Christ— Lk 9:11b-17

Most Sacred Heart of Jesus—Lk 15:3-7

ORDINARY TIME

1st Sunday—See Baptism of the Lord, above

2nd Sunday—Jn 2:1-12

3rd Sunday—Lk 1:1-4; 4:14-21

4th Sunday—Lk 4:21-30

5th Sunday—Lk 5:1-11

6th Sunday—Lk 6:17, 20-26
7th Sunday—Lk 6:27-38
8th Sunday—Lk 6:39-45
9th Sunday—Lk 7:1-10
10th Sunday—Lk 7:11-17
11th Sunday—Lk 7:36—8:3
12th Sunday—Lk 9:18-24
13th Sunday—Lk 9:51-62
14th Sunday—Lk 10:1-12, 17-20
15th Sunday—Lk 10:25-37
16th Sunday—Lk 10:38-42
17th Sunday—Lk 11:1-13
18th Sunday—Lk 12:13-21
19th Sunday—Lk 12:32-48
20th Sunday—Lk 12:49-53

21st Sunday—Lk 13:22-30
22nd Sunday—Lk 14:1, 7-14
23rd Sunday—Lk 14:25-33
24th Sunday—Lk 15:1-32
25th Sunday—Lk 16:1-13
26th Sunday—Lk 16:19-31
27th Sunday—Lk 17:5-10
28th Sunday—Lk 17:11-19
29th Sunday—Lk 18:1-8
30th Sunday—Lk 18:9-14
31st Sunday—Lk 19:1-10
32nd Sunday—Lk 20:27-38
33rd Sunday—Lk 21:5-19
34th Sunday (Our Lord Jesus Christ, King of the Universe)— Lk 23:35-43

MAJOR FEASTS OF THE YEAR

Feb. 2: Presentation of the Lord —Lk 2:22-40
Mar. 19: St. Joseph, Spouse of the Blessed Virgin Mary—Mt 1:16, 18-21, 24a or Lk 2:41-51a
Mar. 25: Annunciation of the Lord— Lk 1:26-38
June 24: Nativity of St. John the Baptist (Vigil)—Lk 1:5-17
(Mass during the Day)—Lk 1:57-66, 80
June 29: Sts. Peter and Paul (Vigil) —Jn 21:15-19
(Mass during the Day)—Mt 16:13-19
Aug. 6: Transfiguration of the Lord— (A) Mt 17:1-9 (B) Mk 9:2-10 (C) Lk 9:28b-36

Aug. 15: Assumption of the Blessed Virgin Mary (Vigil)—Lk 11:27-28
(Mass during the Day)—Lk 1:39-56
Sept. 14: Exaltation of the Holy Cross—Jn 3:13-17
Nov. 1: All Saints—Mt 5:1-12a
Nov. 2: Commemoration of All the Faithful Departed (All Souls' Day) 1st Mass—Jn 6:37-40 2nd Mass—Jn 11:17-27 3rd Mass—Jn 14:1-6 (Other Gospels may be used)
Nov. 9: Dedication of the Lateran Basilica—Jn 2:13-22
Dec. 8: Immaculate Conception of the Blessed Virgin Mary— Lk 1:26-38